BE STILL AND LISTEN

Ghitana W. Franklin

Printed in the United States of America

ISBN 979-8-89114-203-9 (sc)
ISBN 979-8-89114-204-6 (hc)
ISBN 979-8-89114-205-3 (e)

Library of Congress Control Number: 2025912947

2025.07.07

MainSpring Books
5901 W. Century Blvd
Suite 750
Los Angeles, CA, US, 90045

www.mainspringbooks.com

Acknowledgement and Thanks

First I have to thank God, who made all things possible. To my husband, Rickey Franklin, I thank you for letting God change your life. To my mother, Annie Williams. Words cannot describe what you mean to me. You have gone beyond the duties as my mother. I am grateful, and I thank God he gave me you. Love You Momma! To my mother-in-law, Arnola Franklin. You don't say much, but your actions speak volumes to me and I thank you and love you. To my children, Philamenia Kirskey, Kierstin Fair and Kaelin Franklin. I am so proud of all of you. Much love to you all. To my sisters, Chelesa Hill and Doris Jackson, and my brother Enrico Chappell. All of you are special to me, and I appreciate each of you for being there in my time of need. God bless, and I love each of you. To my dear cousin Kenosha Hurst. You have been good to me. All I can say is thank you. You are well appreciated. To a special couple in my life, Eddie and Machell Sanford. You are two genuine beings and I appreciate what you both bring to our family. Finally thanks to all the men and women who are standing in the gap for their families; interceding for others when you are going through turmoil yourself. Stay encourage. this book will lift your spirits and make you hope again.

I pray this book will lift your spirits and make you hope again.

*S*pecial *D*edication

I am dedicating my book to all women- black, brown, white, Hispanic, Asian, etc., who have been abused emotionally, sexually or physical. The pain, anger and hopelessness that you may be feeling or have felt will only intensify the hurt and shame, if you do not understand that you cannot fix the situation in your own strength or power. Your way may lead to unforgiveness, which will eventually lead to anger and bitterness- causing a deep hole in your soul, a void in your life; no matter how successful or whole you may think you are. True healing begins when forgiveness starts. The forgiveness is not for the person. You may not think one deserve forgiveness. The forgiveness is for you. It's for your peace, joy and healing. You deserve these things. This is the way I looked at my situation instead of just going through, I have grown through. You might be crying now, but there is a better day for you. I learn obedience, sacrifice, and discipline from the things I suffered in my life. Three words I asked...God help me!

My poems are my story. They are raw, but real.

God Bless

She thought it was about the fight for her marriage.
In actuality, it was about the fight for her soul, her very life.
She had to be still & listen to come to this revelation.

Be still and know that I am God...
Psalm 46:10 (KJV)

In the midst of the storm, the pain, and the hurt,
God is always there. He just wants you to be
still and listen. When you do, He will give
you...

Beauty for ashes
Joy for your mourning
Hope for the hopelessness
Peace that surpasses all understanding
Healing for your brokenness
Calm from your storm
Grace that is sufficient
A light to guide you
Strength for you weakness
Courage to overcome
Help in the times of trouble
Jesus for Your Answer

Contents

Despair & Hopelessness

"Come to Me, all you who labor and are heavy laden, and I will give you rest. Take My yoke upon you and learn from Me, for I am gentle and lowly in heart, and you will find rest for your souls. For My yoke is easy and My burden is light."

Matthew 11:28-30, NKJV

"We are hard-pressed on every side, yet not crushed; we are perplexed, but not in despair; persecuted, but not forsaken; struck down, but not destroyed."

2 Corinthians 4:8-9, NKJV

"Therefore we do not lose heart. Even though our outward man is perishing, yet the inward man is being renewed day by day. For our light affliction, which is but for a moment, is working for us a far more exceeding and eternal weight of glory, while we do not look at the things which are seen, but at the things which are not seen. For the things which are seen are temporary, but the things which are not seen are eternal."

2 Corinthians 4:16-18, NKJV

"Casting all your care upon Him, for He cares for you."

1 Peter 5:7, NKJV

There are times in life
I do have doubts.
Times in my life
I don't know what it's all about.

When I try to sit and discuss
It all ends in a fuss.
We need to get pass this
Or can it be something I already missed.

You keep telling me there is nothing wrong
God keep saying child leave this alone.
Why is that so hard to do?
I'm just trying, I'm trying to get through.

He can tell when I'm on tense
He kicks in on the defense.
Please help me control my emotions
Oh Father! Help me understand this man's notion.

Being married without being love is...
Like having a God without the heavens above.
A relationship takes two
Some TLC will surely do.

A healthy marriage is one I seek,
God is the One who does the keep.
Please stop taking me for granted
You reap the seeds that are planted.

Be careful of what you sow,
Certain things you don't want to grow.
I want life to give me what I give,
Not to survive, yes live
No one wants to be treated wrong,
Be mindful take care, care of your own.

Like a hard nut needs a hoe
Not a hammer.
He doesn't understand
Understand my grammar.

Put no time and effort into me
Not even a card under the Christmas tree.
Is this marriage of no means?
I sure don't feel like your Queen.

I know what kind of woman I am
God has a thing in a bush called a Ram.
You said asked God for a good wife
He gave you a woman in love with Jesus Christ.

While riding in my car I sit and stare
Up in the clouds, oh I want to be there.
So much freedom in the sky
No more tears in my eye.

No more chains on my feet
Some days all I have done, done is weep
I want to escape the things
I know I choose to let the anger, let it go.

I need to take time just for me
What is it that I want to see?
God's hand of favor resting on me
A super natural blessing only comes from He.

All I want was to live
Now I do understand your will
As for him and as for me,
We need the cord that makes three.

When I got married the ceremony was calm
No one in a hurry.
The only two guests were Paulette
And Shirley.

Two young
ladies who stood by me
Genuine friends.
I needed
No one to see.

I don't remember that day
Only the moment.
Oh my, was it a sign of an omen?

Almost twenty years have passed away
Why did he marry me
Marry me that day?

When I asked he had no answer
He was full, filled with rancor.
He had deep strife for his ex-wife
Oh Lord, what have I done to my life?

You gave me signs and I did ignore
Give me one more chance
To be adored.

Lord please forgive me for I was bad,
The man I married made me sad.
I engaged in things wasn't nice, he already
Had, yes he had a wife

Yes I must tell, I must tell the truth
When I grow up I want to be like, like Ruth.
The Bible says you reap what you sow
Please be careful and know what you know.

Young with milk still behind my ears never thought
I would shed so many tears.
He was bitter as he could be
Made me think, think it was me.

There is no excuse for my actions
Is that's why I get not satisfaction.
What I did was wrong enough
God please remove these hand cuffs.

Forgive me master for I have sinned.
One day
I hope for all hearts
All hearts to mend

Standing here waiting at the door, oh it hurts
It hurts to the core.
You enter the home I'm down and depressed
Why are you wondering
When it's you who caused the mess.

Without communication where will this end
At the courthouse where it all begin.
Let's talk and ger this thing straight
No it can't, it can't wait.

Can we get clear clarity on our needs?
God said you are head please take the lead.
Never give me reason to look else where
I just might find it find it there.

Take my hand let's go and pray
God grant us peace before we lay.
We want you here right in the center
Our door is open please
come in, enter

Peace in my mind seem so far away
Can't see the light, light of day.
I began to rub my hands together
Time has stop no not forever.

Caught up desperate don't know what to do
Speak to this thing is what I told you.
Rest for my soul is what I need
I will follow Lord if you will lead.

Yes I got myself in a bind right here
I need peace, peace in my mind.
Holy Spirit speak, oh speak what you may
I will listen to what you have to say.

Do you remember I answered your
Prayer before when I
Knocked it was you who answered the door.

I saw the storm comin' as it
Creep, cried Lord, Lord
Help me
I need some sleep.

Tossed and turned my soul
Got weak, take the pain
Please take, take for keep.

Calm my child for this I know
I am the God who runs the show.
Whatever you need I told you to ask
This is just, just one more task.

All things work together for my good
Never want to be misunderstood.
Jesus whispered I'm always on post.
I thank God for Him and the
Sweet Holy Ghost.

A scoop of ice-cream, what's your favor?
A scoop of love, in need of a Saviour.
Lord, you see what I'm going through
It's no way I would win, if it weren't for you.

Did I create this hell for me?
Or is this the kind of hell that must be?
Some hell we cause some we don't.
What kind of hell do you want?

Hell is not a place I want to be
Had my hell, hell on earth you see.
Take this stain, take it from me
I want to get lost like the leaves on top of a tree.

God gave a gift that keeps on giving
It is He who makes my life worth living.
So I'll wait in this pain, this misery
Because I know, I know He has me.

Disappointed & Frustrated

"My thoughts are nothing like your thoughts," says the Lord. "And my ways are far beyond anything you could imagine. For just as the heavens higher than the earth, so my ways are higher than your ways. thoughts higher than your thoughts."

Isaiah 55:8-9

"For I know the plans I have for you," says the Lord. "They are plans for good and not for disaster, to give you a future and a hope."

Jeremiah 29:11

"Don't worry about anything instead, pray about everything Tell God what you need, and thank him for all he has done."

Philippians 4:6

"Do not be anxious about anything, but in everything by prayer and supplication with thanksgiving let your requests be made known to God. And the peace of God, which surpasses all under- standing, will guard your hearts and your minds in Christ Jesus."

Philippians 4:6-7

Time has been lost money can't pay the cost
Count it up, can it all fit in one cup?
The hands of time never go back
We need to get the issues of the rack.

Yes we need time together
This will not go on, go on forever.
Time to sit and talk, if you stop running
You can begin to walk.

Why are you afraid, do you want
To meet the man, the man God made.
You can't continue to ignore.
Things like this will surely get you at the core

I had to sit and take a good look at
Oneself, in every area of my life.
I want health and I want wealth.

So many valleys don't remember the peaks
So much pain makes one weak.
I have a lot of time on my hands
Time to seek the master's plan.

You made promises once a week
Promises made not one to keep.
Stop saying things you're not going to do
Stop and just be honest, be true.

God say He will restore the years
Oh the canker worm have left me in tears.
I surrender my life to you
Is it any value to one who said I do?

I am here trying to survive,
Lord knows I want my life to thrive.
What I see is very real, satan has come, come
For the kill, he can never stop, stop God's will.

Please stop running sit down
And listen did you tell me
Would take your position.

There are issues you need to: address
There are things I will protest.
God said you could take the lead
How can I help if I don't know what you need?

I've been down this road three times before
I find myself back at my mother's door.
There's no one who understand,
Lord I'm just trying to help, help this man.

I believe in you, the things is
Do you believe too? It's never
To late the time is now it's up to you
To ask God how.

Sometimes I laugh, sometimes I cry
Sometimes I do nothing but try.
Try holding this thing together
I thought it would last, last forever.

I'm so ready, ready for whatever
If I'm holding you please tell me never.
You have two wings you can fly
Open your mouth and say bye.

What you say and what you do?
Don't line up, you have to choose
To pass all of your cups.

I want what you want for yourself
Jesus sitteth at the right and not the left.
When we repent He will forgive, for He
Gave one life, one life to live.

The day I became your wife
The day I lost my life.
You are my husband you must try
I thought we were partners until the day we die.

I want to run, run so fast
But I can't live, live in the past.
Lord it seems to follow me everyday
What can I do nothing but pray.

Your feelings and emotions you never
Show, are you that stubborn to
Let it all go. We have lost so much
Time being selfish is sure not a crime.

Never thought my life would
Be like this.
Things you never had
Can't be missed.

It's ok not to want this anymore.
God's peace be with you
When and if you walk out the door,

I have lived this life for so long
I began to wonder what's right, and what's wrong.
Your issue became family issues.
I have gone to God with my petition.

We must deal with this before we go on
We have live a life of all wrong.
I want to see a change in you
I know that I must change too.

You are suppose to cover me
I get more shade from the pecan tree.
The head of your house, a priest in your home
First we must have one of our own.

Jesus yoke is easy, his burdens is light
Your way is hard, his way is right, this is a mess
May I suggest a quest, a quest in search for the one above,
He is our only and First Love.

Hurt, Angry & Unforgiveness

"The Lord is near to the brokenhearted and saves the crushed in spirit."

Psalm 34:18

"Weeping may last through the night, but joy comes with the morning."

Psalm 30:5

"And God shall wipe away all tears from their eyes; and there shall be no more death, neither sorrow, nor crying, neither shall there be any more pain: for the former things are passed away."

Revelation 21:4

"Dearly beloved, avenge not yourselves, but I rather give place unto wrath: for it is written, Vengeance [is] mine; I will repay, saith the Lord."

Romans 12:19

"The LORD is my rock and my fortress and my deliverer, my God, my rock, in whom I take refuge, my shield, and the horn of my salvation, my stronghold."

Psalm 18:2

"Forbearing one another, and forgiving one another, if any man have a quarrel against any even as Christ forgave you, so also do ye."

Colossians 3:13

You always stood behind the scene
Didn't want people to know you were mean.
Sometimes you didn't want me around
When I talk you didn't make a sound.

It's wrong for you to ignore me, It's wrong
To let the children see. You were mean to all
Of us in you we did to trust. You don't care
What you do, why it has to be all about you?

There are things you must know
Things to make your family grow.
Get in front and take the lead
The kids and I will support the need.

Through the things I suffered I learn
Obedience and a cup full of love are the main ingredients.
I will love you until the day I die
Jesus, He is the only reason, the only reason why.

Lord I thank you for my life
Had no clue I would become a wife.
From where I stood I couldn't see
None of those things were in front of me.

Marriage is a give and a take
Yes we do, we do make mistakes.
God want the best for the both of us
Do you know how you lost my trust?

I became the life I live
I got use to what you give.
What I say have you so confused
I am the one who been abused.

The man of God said things you tolerate
You can't change.
Your behavior will not make me deranged
I thought hard and I do see clear
There's nothing in my life that I do fear.

You told me love me had my back
Why do I feel my life has been on attack?
How did this one
My heart had to be guarded.

The more I give the more you take
I'm so glad God took away the hate.
What goals have you met?
Sorry there are no goals you have set.

Material things I never press you for
Is it that you want to walk out the door?
Your action speaks volume to me
I don't like what, what I see.

There are resources in front of you just
To lazy to follow, to follow through.
Let love cast out all your fears.
The time for you have come, come near
You cannot run because you heard God said,
Not one more, one more year.

I sit and cry in the night
Do you care I am in a fight?
It's as though you block it out
I am silent but I need to shout.

I am weight down like blocks on a string
Fear of what tomorrow, tomorrow will bring.
There is no comfort in what you say
I need you to walk Jesus way.

The pastor said life was not design
To be endured I want to live a life
That is secured. God say you are
The house provider told you
The benefits of being a tither.

Has it ever dawned on you Jesus the
Only way to get us through.
I want to see us prosper, to see us grow
What kind of seed must we sow?

How can I relate to you when
I sit in the church pew.
Pastor begins to read my mail
God and I know what it entails

You sit and have no mercy on me
With a close mind and cold heart you will never see
Your issues, my issues, for we all have some
Are yours so big they have made you numb?

Love, peace, and a sound
Mind He gave to us these are
The spirits with more than a plus.

Take your issues along with God's hand
Put trust in the master with the plan.
Draw nigh to Him He always on ready
Those words of His keep us steady.

Seeking, Finding & Trusting

"I lift up my eyes to the hills. From where does my help come? My help comes from the LORD, who made heaven and earth."

Psalm 121:1-2

"But seek ye first the kingdom of God, and his righteousness; and all these things shall be added unto you."

Matthew 6:33

"Trust in the LORD with all your heart, and do not lean on your own understanding. In all your ways ac- knowledge him, and he will make straight your paths."

Proverbs 3:5-6

"Do not let your hearts be troubled. Trust in God; trust also in me."

John 14:1

"Blessed is the man who trusts in the LORD, whose trust is the LORD."

Jeremiah 17:7

"We do not look at the things which are seen but at the things which are not seen. For the things which are seen are temporary, but the things which are not seen are eternal."

2 Corinthians 4:18

"You keep him in perfect peace whose mind is stayed on you, because he trusts in you."

Isaiah 26:3

How do I break from the things I know?
How do I find ways to grow?
There is rest, rest for the weary
Sometimes my days are a bit dreary.

I don't want relations, I want relationship
I need this script, this script to flip
I want everything God said I could have
Put it in reach so I can grab.

I have wasted so much time, the second part
Of my life will be just fine.
With one to share or with one not, I do
Take pleasure in Jesus being all that I got.

Choices I chose, the decisions I made
Jesus was always there at my aid.
I talk about the life I want to live
Thank you God for the life that you give.

I do know where my priorities lie
Lord I'm so tired of just getting by.
The day has come, come to be
What is my next, next for me?

When there were no pennies to rub
Together, I didn't give up no not ever.
My mind been drained like a rack fill
With dishes, we will sit and address all these issues.

I am not a perfect mother or a perfect wife
Nor a perfect servant to the one who gave me life.
Twenty plus years is a long time
Don't has change to I do mind.

Can you see what I see God please
Keep a hold, a hold on me.
Do you know where you
Are going? God is the One, the One all knowing.

I want to eat the fruit of my labor
In need of God to show me some favor.
I've tried hard to make things right
To look at my kids make me continue to fight

There are mountains I must climb
Your favor will save me so much time.
So many things I need to learn
I need things, things to turn.

I am a dreamer living here on earth
Tell me God what I am really worth.
You gave me a pair of wings to fly
I want to soar with the eagles high in the sky.

My life depends on no one else
I do have concerns about myself.
It's not my will or my way please hear me Lord
When I bow to pray.

As I looked back over my life
The hardest thing was to be
My husband's wife. No I didn't understand
Yet it was I who chose the man.

Dark has once again turn to day
Lost for words don't know what to say.
Time is passing, passing us by
He wants to know why do I always cry.

His heart is close to what I'm feeling
That is not so not appealing. I need to talk
I want to know what you are thinking
It's important cuz' our marriage is sinking.

With God we can't fail without God
We've been going through hell. There are things
Staring you right in your face. Take time solve them take your
place.

Heavenly Father you who sits on high
I need to ask a question, a question why?
Jesus said his burden is easy yoke is light
Lord why have I tossed and turned all night

I am fit to be tired of this same old fight
Will you join me not mine but your might
Satan is never on stand by he can't be still
If you don't stop him who will

I am calling, calling on your name
Like the blind the deaf and the lame
Time I know bring about change
My life I tell you been a bit strange.

There is a praise always on my lips
Jesus say sis take this Holy tip
God already know the end of this thing
Take flight, fly, spread your wings.

This morning I wake waiting on your answer
Fear has spread, spread like cancer.
For there is no balance, balance I see
Lord give me means, means to take care of me.

What's my purpose why was I born?
Mentally tired, weak and torn. I refuse
To die and go to hell sometimes
I need to talk, I need to tell.

I began this journey years ago
Yes I've been down been down low.
Can't stop I can't stop now
Jesus is the know and the how.

Here I sit quiet, quiet as a mouse, come on
In Lord come in this house. There are
Three things in this life I need most
My Father, His Son and His Holy Ghost.

Today is here
Wonder what tomorrow will bring.
Sadness, madness
All those horrible things.

Precious is the life God has given us
Be thankful why fuss.
His plan, your plan, He lets us choose
With His plan you will never loose.

Meekness, kindness is a part
Love and laughter is where
We can start.

Ask seek knock watch it
All unfold for God is the
Father of all untold.

Waiting on you Lord waiting to see
When are you coming, coming for me?
Be still, still my child I only need
To test you for a little while.

I trust you Lord, trust you with my life
Take the bitter take the strife.
No man, woman or child can see the
Master plan, the plan you have for me.

Toils and trials you go through
I made you for me not for you.

Hope deferred makes the heart sick
You always gave me a chance to pick.
Wait and wait I did what you said
Thank you Lord for given me a place
To lay my head.

Wishing and wanting for all things now.
God said wait my child need to prepare
You for the know and the how.

Be patient in this, wait for I need you
To participate. For it is I who know the
Way and I who plan all the day.

Listen my child at what I
Say you always can ask
What you may.

Trust in God
Please, please do.
I know He will always
Come, come through.

Healing & Peace

Then shall light break forth like the morning, and your healing (restoration and the power of a new life) shall spring forth speedily; your righteousness (your rightness, your justice, and your relationship with God) shall go before you [conducting you to peace and prosperity], and the glory of the Lord shall be your rear guard."

Isaiah 58:8

"The thief does not come except to steal, and to kill, and to destroy. I have come that they may have 10, and that they may have it more abundantly"

John 10:10

"Peace I leave with you, my peace I give unto you not as the world giveth, give I unto you. Let not your heart be troubled neither let it be afraid."

John 14:27

"The LORD make his face shine upon you and be gracious to you; the LORD turn his face toward you and give you peace."

Numbers 6:25-26

"I will lie down and sleep in peace, for you alone, 0 LORD, make me dwell in safety."

Psalm 4:8

And we know that God causes everything to work together for the good (those who love God and are called according to his purpose for them."

Romans 8:28

Can I fix this can I not?
God's know I did give it my
Best shot. How can I fix it not knowing
What's wrong? Sit down shut up
And leave this alone.

God didn't tell you He needed
Your help, you don't know you're right
From your left. His will His way
Make my day, my gain His glory
My life story.

His test my quest
In search of His best.
His Son my Saviour, yes I'm in
Need of God's favor.

His strength His power I need
every hour. His love and His grace
I need in my place.
I want the blessings you promised me
I love the person who I became to be.

Joy in my life is not far away
The pain in my life can't stay.
It eats at the core of my soul
I can't let my heart, my heart grow cold.

How can I be lonely in my life?
I do have a husband who calls me his wife.
I want to let my hair down
Take off my shoes and do away with the frown.

Freedom, freedom I scream for, oh my
Father please open, open up a door.
I will share, share my brother's wealth
Healing is the best of all best of all health.

The life I live the things I see.
Can there be another life for me?
I dream of peace and happiness
God I know you have already given me your best.

I want what's best and I want it now
Time has force me to seek how.
My life is dead need it to come alive
I want hope I need my life to thrive.

I blame no one for things that happen
To me, I am not a fool I just couldn't see.
Lord help me! Change the way I think
I want to change the way I live, always
Teach my heart please to forgive.

To do what you do I had to enable you to
See what you see you are not looking at me.
Fear that my peace depended on you
Was I really that numb to think that could be true?

In this marriage there are issues
Do you see the empty box of tissues?
We have one life to live it's not
Always to take but also to give.

It took all these years just to see
What I have done, done to me.
I took my eyes off God's Son
I ask myself what was the reason.

I became focus on the man I married
He and the baggage that he carried.
I cannot, cannot fix this man
There is not one human who can.

His issues has become my issues and
It is a mess. I have to look to God who only know
Know best. I will continue to search until I am
Satisfied the truth will come if there are any lies.

I grew up with my father not around
Sometimes I wonder where he could be found.
He gave me no instruction, no directions
Not even once did he give me corrections.

For a long time I hated my father he left me
Nothing didn't even bother.
I had to learn how to forgive, this
Is my life I want to live?

If you have done, done all you can
Even reach out to grab his hand.
He might not ever, ever reach back
You are not responsible for the way he act.

You can't change him only God can
Seek him for he know, he know the man.
Give this to me and let it go
Prayer for him can change his flow.

Speak Lord oh speak to me
My soul is tired please set it free.
Like a dark cloud in the sky my heart is
Heavy and I do know why.

So many valleys I just need to see the peak
It's God who I must, who I must seek.
The enemy all up in my ear
God didn't give me the spirit, the spirit of fear.

Love, peace, and a sound mind satan
The devil refuses I say refuses to be kind.
To kill steal and destroy don't play
With him he is not a toy.

Cast all your cares on the one above
He is the one who is full of love. Rest for my
Soul and a heart that is light
God's word can and will give, give you sight.

What I done cause me so much pain
I am the one who the blame.
I did have an affair with a married man
could it be I should have, I should have ran.

I had no respect for this
Woman's his wife, feelings.
I really didn't think this would be so revealing.

Day by day listening to what
He had to say, I did not realize
Yes he told, told some lies.

I can't take back what I have done
Surely this will help, it will help someone.
To want a woman's husband is very wrong
I needed to ask God to give me one of my own.

Take my hand Lord guide me your way
Lead me please I need to see a better day.
Teach me how to have faith in you
God help me, help me to make it through.

You broke me to put me back together
You emptied me to fill me forever.
It was you who allowed me to go so low and it
Was you who never let me go.

I love you God I honor you I bless your name
Your Son, my brother, Jesus keeps me sane.
I bless your name
Thank you for your Holy Spirit that lives
In me can't live, live without it "you see."

I raise my hands as I praise your
Holy name. Change me Lord I don't
Ever want to be the same.

I've seen some dark days in my life
Days feel with emptiness, bitterness and strife.
Take this stain, stain from me I am
Your child God I know you see.

Days where I feel so all alone days with
Nothing to call my own.
Time has passed, passed me by
Some days I wanted, I wanted to die.

You told me take courage be strong
Just hang tight hang on.
So I ask the question how much, how much long?

I take my walk with you oh so serious
Sometimes it leaves me quite, quite curious.
I stand, stand on your word.
In time of need it was you, you who I heard

Than you Lord for all you do.
It took time but I grew
You took the days filled
With emptiness, bitterness and strife
Now I can live a long, good, godly
And healthy life.

All things are possible with
The God we serve.
He always given us
Things we don't deserve.

Wake up see the Master at
His plan remember this
Whole world is in His hand.

Be patient wait I say on me for
This you too will see.
Speak and decree a thing to be
For Jesus spoke to the fig tree.

Form your world this power
I gave to you, take my hand
And lets walk this thing through.

This morning I woke out of my sleep
Casting all cares on the one who keeps.
On my knees must I go finding
The peace, peace I know.

God to His arms around ine
All the day.
Leading me
Guiding me all the way.

Words that calm, calm, my soul.
Giving me warmth where
There is cold.

Thank you Lord thank you
For this day, Jesus said
No more price, price to pay.

Storms in my life were raging like the sea
Peace be still
For I know God is with me.

The weight on my shoulder
The hurt in my heart
Anxiety, depression was all a part.

As I sit and stare my Father say to me
Child be of good courage
For I am with thee.

A praise on my lips, a song in my heart
Don't ever give up on God
For He has already done His part.

The depth of my depravity runs
Deeper than I know the hate
The grief it all began to show.

Wonder why so much pain in me
Suppress so long I thought it was gone.
A time to heal is all I ask
My Father said another, yes another task.

I heard a voice say please don't fret
I made you for me don't you forget.
Help me Father help me please
Never to let this become a disease.

Wisdom is from up above, do you
Know, know about God's love.
Lead me Lord, lead the way
One more step is what I say.